The Ambitious Chick's Guide to:

# DISCOVER YOUR SOUL'S MISSION

TAMARA WAMSLEY

ISBN-13: 979-8-3859-7817-5

# CONTENTS

# WELCOME

It was 2012 and I was so miserable in my job that I was having multiple panic attacks each day. It got to the point that I was waking up in the middle of the night with my heart pounding and fluttering like crazy. I was working a full-time job that was taking 11 hours out of each day, Monday through Friday.

I had 3 kids and I still did not know what I wanted to be when I grew up. I knew I had to make a change. But I felt stuck. Inside I had so much ambition, but I had no clarity on what I wanted and ZERO desire to climb the corporate ladder. I felt confused and trapped.

This past decade has taught me a lot about myself. I have come to believe that each of our souls are sent here on a mission. I believe that we are each assigned to do work that only we can do, and that we are given our talents, strengths, and personality to support our mission.

I believe that I felt the way that I did because the job that I had at that time was not in alignment with my soul's mission. I was going through the motions each day, but I was not living the life I was meant to be living, and my soul was screaming at me to change. But now, I've found the process that I needed in order to find clarity.

Now, I am blessed to empower bold, ambitious women like you! As a coach, I get to help you find the freedom and fulfillment you crave! And I ABSOLUTELY FREAKING LOVE IT! I remember the first time I heard about Bronnie Ware and her book, *The Top Five Regrets of the Dying*. I was struck that the #1 regret people have at the end of their life is:

*"I wish I'd the courage to live a life true to myself, not the life others expected of me."*

That statement brought me to tears! In that moment, I knew that was what I was doing! And, I swore I would change it. I do not want to have that regret when I am on my death bed!

AND, I DON'T WANT YOU TO HAVE THAT REGRET EITHER!

- *Tamara*

# YOU ARE WORTH IT!

Commit to yourself.

We often do not give ourselves the same courtesy that we give to others. If you had a friend that promised to do something with you and then she didn't show up, how would you feel about her? And yet, we do this to ourselves all the time. Not anymore. You love yourself and you aren't going to let yourself down anymore, right?

I would like to ask you to make a commitment to complete this course, right here, right now. Promise yourself that you will complete every exercise. Pledge to be 100% honest. That you will let the truth come out, even when it makes you feel uncomfortable. You do not have to share this workbook with anyone. Promise to be completely authentic. Let's set a complete-by date to hold ourselves accountable. If you agree, complete the following:

I [name] _____ promise to complete every exercise in this course to the best of my ability by [date] _____ .


Sign: _____


YAY! That is so exciting! You my friend, deserve to be HAPPY!

We only get one life! We deserve to live the life of our dreams! Why on earth do we live the life that others expect instead of going for what we really want?

Negativity blocks change. Do not allow negativity to keep you stuck!

**Affirmation (print this and place it where you can repeat daily):**

*I release the limiting beliefs that are holding me back from achieving my soul's mission. Today, I fully step into the pursuit of what my soul desires. I appreciate what makes me different from others. I take action! I am worthy of living my best life!*

How does saying those words make you feel?

# FINDING YOUR PURPOSE

*"You can't go back and change the beginning, but you can start where you are and change the ending."* —C.S.Lewis

## WHERE ARE YOU NOW?

What do you do for a living?

Why do you do what you do?

Rate what you currently do:

- ☐ Love it
- ☐ Like it
- ☐ Tolerate it
- ☐ Dislike it
- ☐ Hate it with a passion

Are there parts of what you do that you enjoy? If so, which parts do you like:

In your job, do you help anyone? Who do you help?

Do you like helping this group of people?

# LEARNING ABOUT IKIGAI

In the U.S. educational system, we are taught to choose a career based on what we see others doing around us. We are expected to find a career outside of ourselves. Very early in childhood, we are asked what we want to be when we grow up. A doctor? A lawyer? A teacher? What your parent does for a living? We are given lists of career examples and areas of study to choose from. It is no wonder that so many of us live decades of our lives without finding out what makes us happy.

In Japan, they believe very differently. They believe that our *Ikigai* is hidden deep inside us and requires an internal search to discover. *Ikigai* is a Japanese word describing a reason for being. Some also explain it as your reason for getting out of bed in the morning.

Studies have shown that the Japanese people who are living their *Ikigai* have the highest percentage of people who live to see their 100th birthday and beyond. Not only do they live longer than most of the world, they are healthier and vibrant into their advanced years. The rate of chronic illness is much lower and they do not suffer from the same menopause symptoms that Americans have come to accept as normal.

The opposite of depression is not happiness—it's *purpose*. I believe that having a clear purpose - your Soul's Mission - creates happiness and reduces the stress in our lives.

Clarifying your *Ikigai* can be life changing.

Let's brainstorm using *Ikigai* principles...

To begin, let's take 3 slow deep breaths and close your eyes for a moment. Open yourself up to positive energy. Focus on what you do want.

This is a brainstorming exercise. Do not edit anything that comes to you. Just write it down. Write it ALL down.

There will be 4 brainstorming topics. You will have 5 minutes for each topic. Set a timer for 5 minutes and brainstorm the first section. Then, repeat for all 4 sections.
Ready?

What do you love to do?

What are you good at?

What does the world need?

What can you get paid to do?

# IKIGAI

*The gold star in the center of the venn diagram is your sweet spot.*

*Look back at your ideas from all four pages.*

*Can you combine any of the ideas that you had?*

*What do you love to do that you are also good at?*

*Then ask yourself, does the world need this?*

*And then, can I get paid to do this?*

We want to select an idea that will check all four boxes.

What ideas do you have that could work? Write them down:

## YOUR WHY

Discovering how you feel is important. Discovering WHY you feel that way, is profound. Your **Ultimate Why** has the power to drive you when you're feeling overwhelmed. **Understanding your why will inspire you and excite you to keep going even in the face of adversity.**

Before we jump in, we need to define your goals. Take a moment to answer a few questions:

Why are you here?

What is the most important thing that you want to accomplish by the end of this workbook?

How are you feeling about your current situation?

What are you hoping to discover?

What is your biggest goal?

Why are you willing to do this work?

How motivated are you to change on a scale of 1-10?

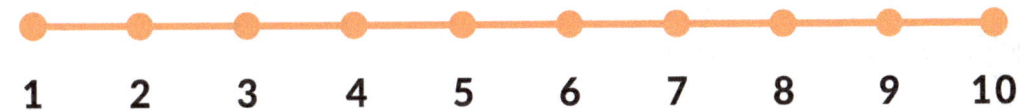

1    2    3    4    5    6    7    8    9    10

What do you want your life to look like 3 years from now?

Let's uncover your WHY.

Let's set family aside for now. Most of us could say our why is our family, and that is a great why, but I have found that we all have another why that comes from deep within us. A mission for our soul to accomplish that is separate from our family, that is just for us.

Do the following exercise with me to see if you can uncover a deeper WHY from your soul.

What will change for you if you clarify your soul's purpose?

Let's dig deeper.

Tell me why that will change?

Keep going, tell me why that is true.

Why?

I know this might seem silly, but trust the process. Keep asking why until you get a really clear vision of your Ultimate Why. Keep going until you are ready to cry.

**Your why will make you cry.**

If you cry, you have likely connected to a deep emotion, which is very good! If you feel this deep emotion, write it down.

Write down what came up for you and what your why might be.

**It matters because YOU MATTER!**

It is that simple. Whatever higher power you subscribe to, you must believe that your God or Universal Intelligence does not make mistakes. Right?

You were chosen. You are here in this moment, in this exact place and time for a reason. You, my friend, are reading this workbook, right this second—for a reason!

I believe that you have a sense that you are made to do something special. Something bigger than what you are currently doing. You are here to achieve Purpose and Prosperity! And guess what? The world is waiting for it too! The Universe is counting on you! Because no matter what your thing is, we need it! We need it to come from you! In a way that only you can do it!

The sad truth is that most people are too scared to dare to do what their soul wants them to do. Most people find themselves at the end of their life regretting not having lived the life that they dreamed about. Bronnie Ware, author of *The Top Five Regrets of the Dying*, says that the number one regret at the end of life is:

*"I wish I'd had the courage to live a life true to myself, not the life others expected of me."*

But you, my dear friend are different. You are brave! You are not going to quit until you get clear on what you want and go for it!

The secret to getting to that point is to keep moving forward, keep trying, don't quit. It won't be perfect in the beginning, and it doesn't have to be. None of us are perfect. Keep trying, keep failing. We just keep learning and gradually we get better.

Channel your inner Dory and "just keep swimming."

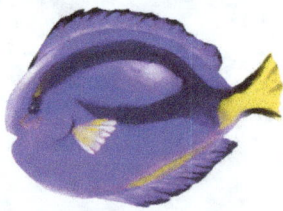

Choosing to take control of your life and being more of your authentic self will lead to more joy in your life almost immediately, simply by putting you in the driver's seat. You're telling yourself and the Universe that you are going to find fulfillment, push through the challenges, and that nothing can stop you.

You are not powerless, you are in complete control. And you are worth it!

What came up for you? Jot it down.

# REFLECTION

Think about what you learned in this module. Journal below with your thoughts and ideas:

*"One of the best things you can do to improve the world is to improve yourself."* —Jen Sincero

## YOUR BIGGEST DREAM

Is there something that you long to do but have told yourself it is not possible? Is there something that you keep thinking about? If you could do ANYTHING in the world, what would it be? What would you do?

Does this question make you uncomfortable? If so, why do you think that is? Is there something that pops into your head that you reject? Do you tell yourself that you can't do that?

Do not edit yourself during this exercise. Let yourself dream. Write it all down. If you still do not know, that is ok. Just continue with the questions, and if you think of something at a later time, come back and write it down.

What excites you? Think about the last time you were speaking to someone and you got excited. What were you talking about? Why did you get excited? What excites you most? What upsets you most?

Let's do a visualization exercise:

Find a place where you can be calm and relaxed. Try to use all your senses. Close your eyes for a moment and take 3 deep breaths. When you are relaxed, take a few minutes to picture your dream life in as much detail as you can. Then answer the following questions about what you were able to see.

In your dream life... Where are you? Who is around you? What are you doing? What do you see? What do you smell? What do you taste? What can you hear? What can you touch? What do you feel? What in this exercise stood out the most to you?

Think back to your childhood.  What did you want to be when you grew up? Make a list:

I believe that when we are little, we are more connected to our soul's purpose, but in a different, more innocent way. Our 7-year-old brains understand the world very differently than we do as adults. When we connect our desires to our 7-year-old lives, we are more creative and we have more faith in our abilities. If we look back deeply, we can uncover very important clues.

For example, I remember taking dance classes as a little girl and saying that when I grew up, I wanted to own a dance studio like the one I took classes in. As an adult, I could not figure out what I wanted to be when I grew up. I struggled with the question for 40 years. Then, one day I had an a-ha moment. I knew at the age of 7 that I wanted to own the business. I had ignored this piece of information for 30+ years! I didn't want to own a dance studio anymore, so I ignored all of that instead of looking deeper. I knew at 7 that I didn't want to be a dance teacher—I wanted to own the place! I began to see that there were clues all around me the entire time. Don't take your childhood dreams literally, like I did.

Take a look back at your list of childhood dreams. Do you see any clues? What do the careers you listed have in common? For example, maybe they all help people or maybe they are all the boss. Did you want to save people? Did you want to travel the world?

Look back at your list. Do you see any clues? Take a moment to note your thoughts:

Next, think of 3 people that you admire most (real, characters on TV, dead, or alive).

Write down your 3 people:

Have your list? Review your list and answer the following questions:

Why do these 3 people stand out to you?

What is it about them that you admire most?

Do the 3 people that you listed have anything in common?

How would it feel to do what they do for a living?

Would you like to do what they do?

Do you want to do exactly what they do or something a bit different?

Maybe you would want to combine what two of them do together?

Do any of the people that you listed help the group of people that you want to help? How do they help? What do they do? What is it about them that makes you admire them? We often admire qualities in others that we want to develop in ourselves.

Do the people in your list give you any clues about your soul's mission? If so, make a note.

Take a few minutes and continue adding to your list of the things you love to do. Is there anything you forgot? Include hobbies, interests, etc. What have you always wanted to try but haven't tried yet?

What is your biggest dream? If you could do ANYTHING and you knew you would be successful, what would you do? Let yourself say it out loud. I will give you a hint... this big dream should be scary. It should be SO BIG that it is embarrassing. You likely have never mentioned it to anyone. If you are thinking of something, go ahead, be brave—say it out loud anyway!

Now, write it down as if you already do it. Like someone just asked you what you do for a living and you are simply answering because it is already true.

If you could only help **one group** of people who would it be?

Be as specific as you can. Want to help kids? Great! What kids?

When you are helping these people, what do they need help with? Close your eyes and imagine yourself helping these people. What does that look like for you? Where are you? What are you doing? What are they doing? How are you helping?

How can you help your group of people to get a transformation.
Fill in the blanks of this sentence:

**I help [insert group of people] go from [point A] to [point B].**

## UNDERSTANDING BEHAVIOUR

Think about this for a moment... The thoughts we think create our emotions. The emotions we feel determine our actions. Our actions create results.

So, if you can control and change your thoughts, you can change your actions. Stick with me for a second, try this exercise:

Take 3 deep breaths and sit quietly for 3 minutes. Don't do anything at all, just sit. Close your eyes. You can even set a timer if you like. When your time is up you can continue reading. Don't cheat. Start now, I'll wait... 3 minutes.... go.

Ok, now tell me... did at least one thought go through your head while you were trying to sit quietly? Whatever the thought was, did you try to think about it? OR were you a separate being that was observing the thought? Ohhh... that's so good isn't it?

Humans often think that we are our thoughts. That we create every thought that pops into our minds but, that is not true. We are the one who is observing our thoughts. We often hear thoughts in our heads because we are the observer, not the one thinking every thought.

If you are the thoughts, then who was just observing them? Learning to be the observer of our thoughts is the first essential step of meditation.

Where do the thoughts come from?

Most of them are from our subconscious programming. I believe that some are from our soul, the Universe, God, whatever title you choose to assign.

Science tells us that 80% of our thoughts are negative and 95% are repetitive—***95%!***

They are often limiting beliefs that keep us stuck where we do not want to be.

When we are trying to find our passion, we get these kinds of thoughts frequently. Most of us dismiss them. Sometimes we do not even realize it's happening at all. Other times, we think, "I can't do that! I'm not **[insert adjective here]** enough."

Or, "what would [insert someone who doesn't pay your bills here] think about me?"

The truth is, we lie to ourselves! We tell ourselves the most hurtful and evil things. If someone else said the same things to us as we say to ourselves, we would feel hurt. But we take it from ourselves all the time! Why do we treat ourselves so harshly?

As you go through this course, I want you to stop dismissing any ideas that come to you, no matter how crazypants they might seem. You don't have to do the thing right now. Just jot it down. Keep a list of everything that crosses your mind.

Do you already know? Is there an idea that keeps coming up? If so, write those down too.

I want to challenge you a bit more. Think about this...

Early in our childhood we begin to form perceptions of the world around us. We take information from our parents, friends, and loved ones, and establish them as facts. How accurate do you think your perception of the world was at age 6? You probably still believed that Santa and superheroes were real, right? How about at age 10?

The fact is that our paradigms that we use as the basis for all our beliefs are inaccurate. Our loved ones might mean well, but they often give us our limiting beliefs. Maybe you had someone tell you that "money doesn't grow on trees" or you will have to "work really hard to make a living." Maybe you had someone tell you that the world is dangerous and not to take risks. Or maybe you had someone tell you that you are stupid, unlovable, or worse.

It is entirely possible that what you heard in your 6-year-old mind was not the message that they even intended to send. And yet, here we are, decades later telling ourselves these same terrible things and believing them!

My point is... we need to question all of it! Every thought, every limiting belief. Nothing from our crazy head should go unexamined.

Take a deep breath.

By taking that breath did you steal oxygen from everyone else?

No. That's not how it works. And, guess what, that's not how other things work either but we have been made to believe that is how the world works.

Love doesn't work like that. Love multiplies! Each time you have a child, they do not share the love you have to give. Your love multiplies.

When you put the energy into exercising, you get more energy back. When you make money, you are not preventing others from making money. Money is energy. Everything including money is abundant. When you give money, you get more in return. It multiplies!

If you want to change your life, you must begin by changing your thoughts, creating new actions, and therefore, new results in your life!

What thoughts do you want to change?

What are your limiting beliefs? Write them down:

Think back to the limiting beliefs you listed above, how can you change them to be positive? Choose a few of the strongest limiting beliefs you listed and write down the opposite affirmative statement.

Here's an example: *There are already people who are successfully doing what I want to do, people will not want to work with me when they could work with them.*

Flip it to the positive: *There are people who have proven that what I want to do is possible, that I can be paid to do this work and how I do it will be different and attract the right clients for me.*

When these limiting beliefs come up again, remember to change them to your positive statement instead.

# HOW DO YOU WANT TO FEEL?

What feeling is the most important to you?

Think about this for a moment. What is the most important emotion to you?

Do you want to feel significant, happy, accomplished, wealthy, inspired, safe, valued, like a hero, or maybe prosperity is your goal? The list of available feelings is unlimited. Take a look at the feelings list in the resource section at the end of this guide and choose one that fits for you.

What is your word?

Understanding what you really want underneath it all will help give you direction. Someone who wants to feel independent is less likely to be driven by helping others. What feeling is it that you really desire?

Understanding how you most want to feel gives you the power to create more of it in your life. Remember, our thoughts create our emotions and our emotions create our actions.

What thoughts do you need to have in order to create the feeling that you most desire? How can you feel more of that feeling? What can you do today to feel your most valued feeling?

Here is an example: *I want to feel significant. It is important to me to make a difference in the lives of others. If I want to feel significant, what action can I take today to make a difference in someone's life?*

**Complete this sentence:**

I want to feel [insert most important feeling]

.

It is important to me to feel [insert most important feeling] because...

I will [insert action]                                              today to make myself

feel [insert most important feeling]

## THE EQUATION FOR CHANGE

People generally avoid loss rather than create improvement in their lives. It is easier to take no risk and remain the same. Change takes effort. I believe that there is an equation for change:

$$D \times V \times E \times C > R$$

Our level of **D**issatisfaction with the current situation

X

our **V**ision for the future

X

how **E**asy it is to take the first step in making this change

X

our level of **C**onfidence in our ability to make the change

must be > (greater than)

our **R**esistance to change.

How much do you really want this?

## REFLECTION

Think about what you learned in this module. Journal below with your thoughts and ideas:

## DEFINING PROSPERITY

What does prosperity mean to you?

What is standard of living?

How would you rate your current standard of living?

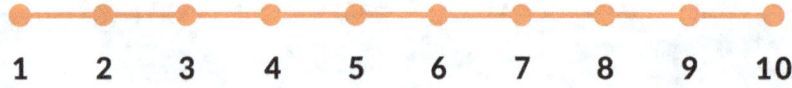

1    2    3    4    5    6    7    8    9    10

What is quality of life?

How would you rate your current quality of life?

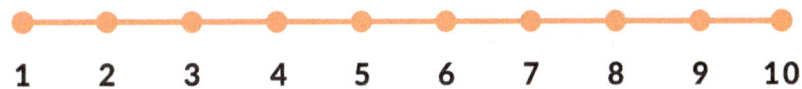

1   2   3   4   5   6   7   8   9   10

What is the difference between the two?

Which one do you feel is more important and why?

To me, standard of living is the ability to financially meet your needs, such as food, shelter, clothing, etc. where as quality of life is the amount of joy you get to experience.

The two are very different.

PROSPERITY = FREEDOM

*"Our fantasies are our realities in an excuse-free world."*

*— Jen Sincero*

## BE LIMITLESS

Adults tend to think a thought, then think "Oh, I could never do that," and delete it before ever really giving it a chance. Children don't do this; they dream without limits.

I want you to be childlike today. Every idea that you have is fantastic. There will be no editing and no deleting. Write down everything that comes to your mind for the following questions. It is ok if you do not have an answer to some of the questions. Maybe something will come to you later. Don't force it. Be kind to yourself.

What have you always dreamed of doing? What is it about that dream that excites you?

What are you afraid to do? Do you have a thought that keeps coming up, but you dismiss it because of your limiting beliefs, the resistance, lack of confidence, or fear?

# WHO DO YOU WANT TO BE?

Who do you want to be?

What do you want people to think of you?

What do you want your legacy to be after you are gone?

## SHARE YOUR EXPERIENCES

What have you survived, learned, or lived through?

What knowledge and experience do you have?

How could you use your experiences to help others?

How would helping them make you feel?

# FLIPPING TROUBLE

What do you do that gets you into trouble?

Let's flip it. Is there a place where doing that thing would help you to be great? How can doing that thing be used for good?

Here is an example: *I used to get into trouble for my big mouth. While working for a corporation, I would not blindly follow the direction of my boss. I would frequently question authority and push back on instructions when their direction did not make sense to me. My co-workers were often appalled by my behavior.*

*The fact is, I was in the wrong role. My ability to stand up and ask questions and challenge the status quo was a huge asset. Just not to that group of people, or in that job. But think about what makes a good activist or attorney, I could kill it in those roles! LOL!*

When we align our work with a position that uses our personality as an advantage (not where you are constantly criticized for it), we can find success much easier and faster.

Where could you be MORE of who you naturally are:

## HELPING OTHERS

In the last 12 months have you helped anyone? How did you help them? Can you list 5 examples of how you have helped others?

## CHAMPION A CAUSE

If you had to choose one cause to work for, what would it be?

## CREATE A PERSONA

Think back to the group of people you most care about helping. Maybe you chose women or children. Maybe you chose a group facing a specific challenge. Try to narrow this down even more. What are they experiencing? What problem do they have? Can you narrow your focus to **one ideal person**? *Hint: The person that you think of could be a previous version of yourself.* How old are they? What problem are they facing? Create an image of the person you most want to help. Now think about what you can offer that would help them. List at least 3 things.

## REFLECTION

Think about what you learned in this module. Journal below with your thoughts and ideas:

*"There are no limits to what you can accomplish, except the limits you place on your own thinking."*
— *Brian Tracy*

I believe your personality was given to you for a reason. I believe that your personality is a huge asset when it is used in the right way. In other situations, it will get you into trouble. This is true for all of us.

## PERSONALITY TYPES

There are many personality tests that you can take online to get a clearer picture of your personality. I have two favorites: **Myers Briggs Type Indicator (MBTI)** and **Enneagram**.

The difference between the Enneagram and Myers Briggs has been described as nature versus nurture. Myers Briggs helps us to understand how we process information. This is the nature side. It is how we naturally behave.

The Enneagram is the nurture side. It helps us to see how we behave under stress and how we subconsciously protect ourselves. It has been described as our go-to strategy for dealing with trauma or *why* we do what we do. Trauma is a strong word. In the case of the Enneagram, it is believed that the first "attack" you faced as a child, no matter how tragic or how minor it may have been, your psyche created a go-to strategy to handle these kinds of situations and this is your primary Enneagram type.

Take the Myers Briggs personality test. If you have already taken it in the past, find your results or re-take the assessments.

## MYERS BRIGGS TYPE INDICATOR (MBTI)

*Get the links to the assessment in the resource section at the end of this guide.*

Make a note of your type and read your Myers Briggs results. What words stand out to you from your test results? Which personality traits resonate with you most? Which ones do you love about yourself? Which ones do you want to use more often?

Take a moment to jot down the highlights of what you have learned about yourself:

*"No matter what happens, no matter how far you seem to be away from where you want to be, never stop believing that you will somehow make it."*

*— Unknown*

Let's take the Enneagram Assessment. If you have already taken it in the past, find your results or re-take the assessment.

## ENNEAGRAM

*Get the links to the assessment in the resource section at the end of this guide.*

Read your Enneagram Assessment results. What is your primary type? What is your wing? What words stand out to you from your test results? Which personality traits resonate with you the most? Which traits do you love about yourself? Which would you want to use more often?

Take a moment to jot down the highlights of what you have learned about yourself:

*"Your always one decision away from a totally different life."*

*— Unknown*

# CLIFTON STRENGTHS

What are your top 5 strengths?

I strongly recommend taking the assessment to get your top 5 if you don't already know them.

*Get the links to the assessment in the resource section at the end of this guide.*

This assessment will show you what your superpowers are! You will find out what you can do with ease that most other people cannot. If you leverage your top 5 strengths in the work that you do every day, you will be a rock star in your work. And, the chances of you having the same top 5 strengths in the same order as someone else is 1 in 33 million!

List your top 5 Strengths:

1.                                          4.

2.                                          5.

3.

Now review your assessment report. What words or phrases in your strengths stand out most to you?

Which parts of your descriptions do you want to do more of every day? What can you leverage to become more successful on your path?

Can you combine two or more strengths to increase your success? What did you learn about your personality?

What do you naturally do well? How can you add more of these behaviors and activities into your daily life?

How can you use your personality and strengths to help others?
When you think about helping other people with your personality and strengths, how does it make you feel?

Can you think of a few careers that best align with your strengths?

What could you do that would use your top strengths every day?

Brainstorm below:

## REFLECTION

Think about what you learned in this module. Journal below with your thoughts and ideas:

*"It is confidence in our bodies, minds and spirits that allows us to keep looking for new adventures."*
— *Oprah Winfrey*

**MODULE 05 OVERCOMING THE MONSTER**

## CONFIDENCE

We envy those we think have more of it than we do. We want it. We wish we could figure out their secret. But the truth is, confidence is simply a result of the thoughts in our heads. Our thoughts might be based on a prior experience but often, they are not. They are just a fear of something new. You can have more confidence by simply changing the thoughts you think.

Let's say you are going to a networking event. As you are getting ready for the event, you are thinking about how scared you are, how intimidating it feels when you walk through the door, and how you always say something stupid. Blah, blah... the thoughts swirl in your head. What do you think your result is going to be when you arrive? Of course your experience will not be positive. You created the negative before you even arrived.

Now pretend and do your best on this one, really visualize it. Go to a place where it is safe and quiet. Close your eyes. Visualize yourself getting ready for the event. You put on your favorite outfit. Your hair and makeup are perfect today! You check yourself out in the mirror as you head for the door. You look fantastic! This is going to be a great event! On the drive, you think about Ms. X, the one person that you want to connect with the most. You come up with the perfect topic to bring up, so the two of you will have a nice conversation. You listen to her as she tells you about a project she is working on right now. You realize that you have a connection that could really help her to be even more successful with her project, and you promise to make the connection to help her out. You make plans to meet for lunch next week. Things went spectacular at the event. As you head home, you feel successful, confident, and you can't wait to meet for lunch next week.

Your state of mind as you walk through the door is the only thing that changed. And guess what? Your state of mind is the only thing that matters! If you have yourself convinced that you are not good at something, you won't be.

Here's a tip that might surprise you. Everyone feels confident in some areas of their life and they lack confidence in others. We all have something that makes us feel intimidated.

What do you feel most confident about and why?

In what area(s) of life do you lack confidence?

Looking back over your life, can you remember an event that may have caused this lack of confidence? Is it possible to change your perspective on that event? Is it possible that your perception of what happened may not be 100% accurate? How can you change your thoughts and self-talk to improve your confidence in this area?

Up to 90% of the thoughts that we have repeat in our heads daily and most of them are negative. Are you creating the negative thoughts that are harming your confidence level?

## THE RESISTANCE

In his book, *The War of Art*, Steven Pressfield speaks of a natural phenomenon that he refers to as The Resistance. He describes The Resistance as a law of nature. Just as gravity is a force that we cannot see that pulls us to the earth, The Resistance is a force that holds us back from change. Any time we try to make a change in our lives, we will feel The Resistance. It is that sense of danger or threat of embarrassment that we feel.

We often stop trying to make a shift in our lives when The Resistance appears. It scares us into believing that our current position is just fine. It is better to play it safe and stay unhappy. Who really gets to feel fulfilled in their lives anyway, right? Who do you think you are? Do you think you are special?

The Resistance is a full-time inner critic that will destroy your ability to achieve your dreams, if you allow it to. Do not give it that power! The key to overcoming The Resistance is to expect its arrival. Now that you know about The Resistance, you can watch for it. Know that this is truly a natural occurrence and that every single person on this planet feels it, hears it in their heads, and must face the decision of how to respond.

Yes, that's right. Every. Single. Person.

So, when [insert your favorite famous person here] does her/his thing that pushes them outside of their comfort zone, they feel it. The only thing that sets us apart from the famous person you thought of is that they felt the Resistance and keep going anyway.  They know that The Resistance is a dirty lying bastard that is trying to keep us stuck in a life that is not our dream. The only way to get to the dream life is to ignore the Resistance and charge on.

The life you dream of is on the other side of The Resistance. Know that when you feel it, you are heading in the right direction!

When do you feel The Resistance? When was the last time you felt The Resistance? Are you feeling The Resistance now? Can you think of previous times that you have felt it and allowed it to stop you? Does The Resistance appear at the same point in each project, for example? If so, it might help you to begin to predict when the dirty bastard will appear so that you can be prepared for it ahead of time and keep right on doing your thing.

*Your desire to change must be greater than your desire to stay the same."*
*— Unknown*

## YOUR MINDSET—THE STARS WILL ALIGN

You have to believe it! If you believe your dream life is going to happen, it will. You have to *REALLY* believe it. You have to feel it in your bones! You have to FEEL the emotion from it. Visualize it right now. Pretend you have already achieved your dream!

What does it FEEL like? Really feel it, as if it is happening right now. Your dream life is not going to just arrive on your doorstep with a bow. You will have to work for it.

The good news is you do not have to have it all figured out. Just do something that will get you moving in (what you think could be) the right direction. Any movement is good, just try something, anything. It is the action that will get you to the right destination. It is easy to get stuck. If you feel unsure of what direction you should be heading in, that is absolutely okay. Just choose a direction and DO IT! Set aside time to work on your goal every day, even if it is just 15 minutes.

As you put in the work, the universe will begin to support you. The stars will begin to align and strange things will happen. You can brush them off as coincidences if you like, but I promise you, they are not. It is like placing an order with the Universe. Don't believe me? Try it! I dare you! Just remember to focus on this first goal and FEEL what it will feel like when you achieve it. Do not worry that this is not the one and only mission that you have. That is what pivots are for. Just pick a direction and go that way. Nothing is written in stone. You can make changes later when you need to. When you are placing an order with the Universe, be as specific as you can. Here is a bad example:

*Me: I want more money.*

*Universe: Ok, here's a penny in the grocery parking lot. Now you have more money.*

Here is a better example:

*Me: I need $2,257 for this specific new couch that I am dreaming of.*

*Universe: The nice and clean lady down the street just bought that couch a month ago and now she has to move. Here's the new couch you wanted, and it's only $500.*

What can you do today to move the needle in the right direction?
List a few ideas of actions you can you take. You got this!

## REFLECTION

Think about what you learned in this module. Journal below with your thoughts and ideas:

""We can change our lives. We can do, have, and be exactly what we wish."
— Tony Robbins

MODULE
06 ALIGNING FOR SUCCESS

## AFFIRMATIONS

Affirmations are positive statements that you repeat to yourself. When repeated daily, they can help you to overcome negative energy, The Resistance, and other obstacles that we allow to prevent us from achieving our goals.

Here are a few examples:
1. I have courage. I am brave.
2. Everything I desire is already within me.
3. I was created to do this.
4. I can. I will. No excuses.
5. My positive energy is pulling my dreams to me.

Create at least 5 affirmations for yourself and repeat them every morning and every night. Effective affirmations create a positive emotion. They should inspire you and make you feel optimistic about your future.

# ENERGY

Energy work may seem a little too woo-woo for some people. It is often easier for people to understand the physical parts of our lives because they are easier to see, and that is what our educational system focuses on.

Just in case this is new to you, I want to help you to see the energy side of your life and to show you how you can use your energy to create the life you want to have.

Have you ever shocked someone by touching them? That's the energy that you always have within you.

Have you ever walked into a room where the people in the room had been fighting, and you could feel the tension in the air? That's energy that you feel.

Have you ever thought about a loved one and then they call you, as if they received your thought? That's energy.

We experience energy all the time.

As a kid, I was taught that everything that takes up space is made of matter. However, this is no longer thought to be true. Now that we have stronger magnification, we can see that the actual makeup of an atom is not matter. It has been discovered that atoms themselves are 99.999999999% empty space full of energy that is in constant vibration.

This means that our world is only .000000001% matter! The other 99.999999999% is energy! So, if our world is actually made up of energy, it makes it a lot easier to understand how focusing on our energy can impact our lives.

We are energetically affected by our environment and the people around us. Likewise, you have the ability to affect everything around you. If you are around negativity, it will be harder to attract positivity into your life. One way to help balance your energy is by moving your body. Just taking a walk or doing yoga can make a big difference. Pick a song that speaks to you and dance. Try it! You will feel your energy shift immediately! Don't know a good song to choose? Try *Better When I'm Dancin'* Meghan Trainor.

What do you need to change so that positive energy can come to you? Choose one thing that you will do today to improve your energy.

*"You get in life what you have the courage to ask for."*

*— Oprah Winfrey*

## MANIFESTING

Manifesting, also called the law of attraction, became mainstream when the book and the movie *The Secret* came out in 2006. Manifesting is about your ability to create any reality that you want in your life by attracting that energy to you.

Here are the 7 steps to manifest everything you desire:

**1. CLARITY** – You will need to start with a very clear vision of exactly what you want.

**2. ASK** – Next, ask for what you want and be extremely specific.

**3. ACTION** – Take action towards your goal. Thoughts without action are just dreams. The Universe requires us to take action. Do one thing today to get you closer to your goal. What is your next right step?

**4. BE GRATEFUL** – Be thankful for everything you receive. Use a gratitude journal.

**5. LIMITLESS** – You must release your limiting beliefs and resistance around your goal. You cannot attract what you desire if you are afraid, are focused on what you lack, or struggling with negative self-talk. You are limitless! You can manifest anything you desire.

**6. ENERGY** – Improve your energy and raise your vibration. The energy you put out into the world will come back to you. What can you do today to create joy in your life and raise your vibration? How do you want to feel this week? How can you give that feeling to others (and therefore attract it back to you)?

**7. FLEXIBILITY** – Be flexible and trust that the Universe is working It's magic to support you. Remember, everything is happening *FOR YOU*, not *to* you. You have to believe!

# VISUALIZATION

Visualization exercises can be powerful. Find a place where you can be calm and relaxed and visualize your dream.

Scientific studies have proven the effectiveness of visualization. For example, you have likely heard of basketball players that practice seeing the ball go in the hoop, but did you know that one study showed that people who went to the gym increased their muscle mass by 30%, and those who did the workout completely in their heads increased their muscle mass by 13.5%!!!

There is no doubt that focusing on what you want can help you to create it. Which is why creating a vision board and putting it where you look at it every day can have a dramatic impact on what you achieve.

# VISION BOARD

Think about your soul's mission. What goals do you need to achieve in order to get there?

Select images online and from magazines that represent what you desire. Use these images to make a collage that represents your mission. Place your vision board where you will see it EVERY DAY.

Each day take time to look at your vision board. Focus on your mission and visualize having already achieved your goals. What does it feel like to have achieved your soul's mission? Take the time to feel those emotions and really pull this energy into your life.

# JOB DESCRIPTION

Use the information that you have learned throughout this course to write your dream job description. Add as many details as you can. Write the job description as if you are writing it for an open position at your company.

Here are a few suggestions:

What is the objective of your dream job? List general responsibilities, describe key tasks, what relationships will be required to be successful in this role?

What are the expected results for you while you are in this role? List the qualifications, experience, training, and skills needed. Will travel be required? What is the pay range? Where is this position located? What is the environment that you will work in?

## CONNECTING THE DOTS

Look back over the exercises in this course and your notes from each module. What did you discover about yourself? Did you find any clues about what you want? What matters most to you? Did you discover your soul's mission?

Do not quit on your dream. So many people give up before they even try simply because they cannot see how they can get to the goal from where they are now. You absolutely can!

The Universe has the absolute power to align and make it happen for you! And, it can happen so much faster than you can imagine.

You must focus on what you want, not on what you do not want. Do not ask yourself if you can do it. Ask yourself HOW you can do it!

If, heaven forbid, one of your most precious loved ones needed emergency surgery that cost $1 million, you would figure it out, right? You only have this one life. You have to go after your dream with that same level of intensity. You can do this!

Now, how can you move the needle in the right direction?

List 5 things that you can do this week to take steps in the right direction.

## REFLECTION

Think about what you learned in this module. Journal below with your thoughts and ideas:

# CONGRATULATIONS!

You completed this guide! That's awesome!

Craft your soul's mission statement to help bring out the best in you.
Keep it short but effective.

*Here are two example formats:*

*I [how you help] [insert persona] to overcome [a challenge] to achieve [insert your soul's mission].*

*I am [insert your soul's mission] for [insert persona] to help them overcome [their biggest challenge] and achieve [your why].*

*Add your soul mission statement to your vision board.*

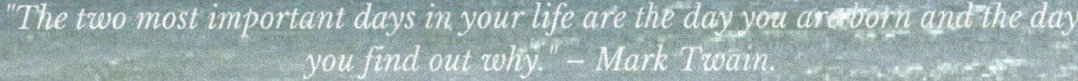

# RESOURCES

## CLIFTON STRENGTHS

Paid official version - https://store.gallup.com/c/en-us/1/cliftonstrengths

Free version - https://high5test.com/cliftonstrengths-free/

## MYERS BRIGGS TYPE INDICATOR

Paid official version- https://www.mbtionline.com/en-US/Products/For-you

Free version - https://www.16personalities.com/free-personality-test

## ENNEAGRAM

Paid official version - https://tests.enneagraminstitute.com/

Free version - https://enneagramuniverse.com/enneagram/test/

# FEELINGS

| | | | |
|---|---|---|---|
| Love | Delight | Forgiveness | Elegant |
| Happiness | Pleasure | Understanding | Graceful |
| Joy | Satisfaction | Respected | Confident |
| Gratitude | Pride | Flexible | Poise |
| Free | Confidence | Adaptable | Composed |
| Contentment | Trusted | Creative | Self-assurance |
| Excitement | Secure | Imaginative | Self-confidence |
| Enthusiasm | Serene | Innovative | Self-esteem |
| Hope | Peace | Ingenious | Self-respect |
| Optimism | Calm | Resourceful | Self-worth |
| Inspiration | Relaxed | Smart | Funny |
| Empathy | Comfort | Intuitive | Playful |
| Compassion | Reassurance | Wise | Amused |
| Generosity | Belonging | Knowledgeable | Entertained |
| Kindness | Included | Growth | Fun |
| Caring | Accepted | Development | |
| Affection | Approval | Progress | |
| Warmth | Acknowledged | Achievement | |
| Admiration | Appreciation | Success | |
| Respect | Recognition | Fulfilled | |
| Adoration | Encouragement | Purpose | |
| Awe | Support | Meaning | |
| Wonder | Motivation | Significant | |
| Amazement | Determination | Gracious | |
| Fascination | Perseverance | Courteous | |
| Curiosity | Patience | Respectable | |

# YOU ARE DESTINED FOR GREATNESS MY FRIEND!

The world is waiting for you to create what only you can create. The world is waiting for you to do what only you can do. We NEED you to fulfill your soul's mission!

**Be Courageous! Go after your dream...It's out there waiting for you!**

# HAVE YOU FOUND CLARITY?
# I WOULD LOVE TO HEAR ABOUT IT!

*Connect with me on social @tamara_wamsley*

# WISH YOU COULD BRAINSTORM IDEAS WITH A PARTNER TO GET MORE CLARITY? SCHEDULE A CALL:

[https://tamarawamsley.com/work-with-me](https://tamarawamsley.com/work-with-me)

Be sure to tune into

# THE AMBITIOUS CHICK PODCAST